Girls Wil

MW00679802

A Book of Quirky Quizzes & Questions—for Girls Only!

Girls Will Be Girls is all about one thing—and one thing only: Being a girl. That means wearing pink or at least not *hating* pink, dreaming of being a princess or dreaming of being a *rock star,* crushing on boys or sticking your nose up at boys, wanting to grow up or wishing you'd stay a kid *forever,* and generally just having goofy, giggly, girly fun with others like you—your best girlfriends! This book isn't a manual on how to be a girl; it's the place where you get to *be* you, exploring your girlhood through dozens of cute quizzes, silly games, quirky questions, and other just-for-fun stuff. Fill it out by yourself or with your friends, over the weekend or during the school year—just do it *your* way, sister!

This book is mine, all mine

Molly Ferguson

That Girl in the Mirror

First things first: Let's get the scoopage on that girl in the mirror there. Hey, wait a sec—that's you! If your life were made into a must-see movie, what would it be like? Here's your chance to find out! Finish your own personal screenplay by circling or writing in the answers for each number. (Pssst! No cheating!!! Don't look at the story on the following pages until you've made ALL your choices.)

1. Choose a title for your film (but remember, *The Princess Diaries* is taken)

_____

2. (Circle one) comedy   drama   action/adventure   sci fi   musical

3. (Circle one) princess   businesswoman   performer   scientist   politician

4. Your pet's name (real or imaginary)_____

5. (Circle one) Cinderella-type   tomboy   cheerleader
                 studious athlete   easygoing student

6. (Circle one) true love   perfect beauty   vacation days
                 girlfriends   school

7. (Circle one) falls in love   saves animals   discovers best friends
                 finds fame   is rescued

8. (Circle one) a wedding celebration   a makeover scene   a road trip
                 a jillion clothing changes   a musical number

9. Choose any two numbers (a) _____   (b) _____

10. (Circle one) girl   teacher   parent   student of any age   grandparent

11. Your all-time fave movie_____

12. Who would you cast as . . .
    (a) You?_____
    (b) Your family?_____
    (c) Your best friends?_____
    (d) Your "love" (or your "like"!) interest?_____
    (e) The supporting roles (teachers, classmates, neighbors, etc.)?_____

    _____

13. Survey says, your movie will be a (Circle one)
    blockbuster hit   summer sleeper   great rental   cool comedy
          powerful drama   total tearjerker   real horror flick

14. Your favorite musician_____

15. Your name_____

16. Your best friend's name_____

17. Your grade level_____

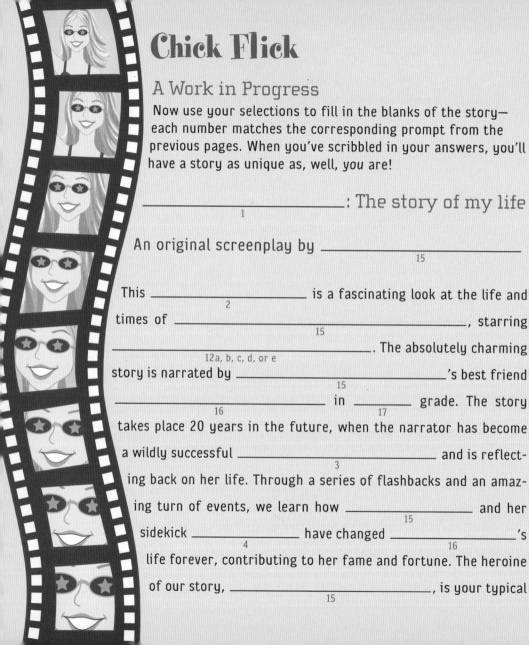

Chick Flick

A Work in Progress

Now use your selections to fill in the blanks of the story—
each number matches the corresponding prompt from the
previous pages. When you've scribbled in your answers, you'll
have a story as unique as, well, you are!

_____: The story of my life

1

An original screenplay by _____

15

This _____ is a fascinating look at the life and

2

times of _____, starring

15

_____. The absolutely charming

12a, b, c, d, or e

story is narrated by _____'s best friend

15

_____ in _____ grade. The story

16   17

takes place 20 years in the future, when the narrator has become

a wildly successful _____ and is reflect-

3

ing back on her life. Through a series of flashbacks and an amaz-

ing turn of events, we learn how _____ and her

15

sidekick _____ have changed _____'s

4   16

life forever, contributing to her fame and fortune. The heroine

of our story, _____, is your typical

15

_____ 5 , but that doesn't stop her from having an extraordinary experience. As the story develops, we learn that _____ 15 treasures her _____ 6 above all else in life, and it's this love that drives her to start on an adventure, during which she _____ 7 . From beginning to end, the story is chock-full of the usual girly escapades and antics. The lead, _____ 15 , is involved in _____ 8 and finds herself in a million tricky tight spots she must extract herself from before the movie ends on a thrillingly positive note—with no fewer than _____ 9a surprise endings, one after the next! We won't give away the finale, but we will say that the story of _____ 15 and _____ 16 is one _____ 13 that no _____ 10 will want to miss. Trust us; it's like a cross between *Titanic* and _____ 11 — a cinematic classic that you'll return to see _____ 9b times! And you *won't* want to miss the amazing soundtrack, with sure-fire hits by _____ 14 .

—*My Chaotic Life*® Press

The Sweetest Thing

Sugar and Spice Quiz

Sure, sugar and spice are nice and everything, but there's more to life than just being a sweetie. Test the stuff you're made of with these sticky situations!

1. Your best friend and you are partners for a totally important school project, and your BFF wants you to do all the work. You

a. do it! It's not THAT hard. And if you get an "A," your BFF will love ya' forever.
b. do it. Despite wanting to teach your bud a lesson, you'd rather get a good grade.
c. throw a hissy fit. You stomp away to let her know what you think of the idea.
d. politely refuse. It's too much work! She can help you or find a new partner.

2. You're hanging out at the mall when your flat broke BFF finds a CD that she says she just can't live without. She asks if you'd buy it for her . . . pretty please? You

a. tell her to forget it. Your cash is your stash, not her own personal piggy bank.
b. buy it. She IS your best friend, and you can save up the green stuff again.
c. deal. You'll buy IF she pays you back. But it's one time only—soul sister or not.
d. tell her to dream on. Why part with your moola for a friend with enough stuff?

3. You're not ALWAYS a klutz, but when you pass a group of older kids at the park, you rollerblade smack into a fire hydrant. You

a. grumble. You make a snide comment and wheel on outta there quick as can be.
b. play it cool. You ask for help and introduce yourself when back on your feet.
c. get up and go. You dust yourself off and get back to your blades, blushing a bit.
d. duck and cover. You can't escape, but you CAN hide for a long, long time.

4. Your parents can be so, well, *parent*-y! When there's an all-school skate party that your parents won't drive you to, you

a. call and cancel. You force a little cough as you explain your sudden illness.
b. decide to walk. (But hope your parents offer a ride before you start the hike.)
c. plead your case. You ask the 'rents if they'd reconsider just this once. Puh-leeze?!
d. phone around. Somebody's gotta have a parent willing to drive, right?

5. You've looked forward to the big school carnival FOREVER! The big day's a week away—but your buds don't plan to go. You

a. decide not to go either. You stay home and fume over your ultra-boring pals.
b. deal with it. You talk some friends into going out to see a movie instead.
c. cry it out. You think about all the fun you're missing between sobs and sniffles.
d. take a stand. You go alone—determined to meet new friends and have fun.

Scoring
1. a = 2, b = 1, c = 4, d = 3
3. a = 4, b = 3, c = 2, d = 1
2. a = 3, b = 1, c = 2, d = 4
4. a = 1, b = 4, c = 3, d = 2
5. a = 4, b = 2, c = 1, d = 3

"Sometimes I'm so sweet
even I can't stand it."
–Julie Andrews, actor

Chocolate
If you scored 5–8 points, you're made of chocolate. You try hard to please, but too much chocolate is never a good thing. Sometimes you've got to take a stand on issues instead of melting down. People will still think it's a treat to know you.

Licorice
If you scored 9–12 points, you're made of licorice. You stand up for yourself— sometimes. You rope in support from your friends, but you bend to pressure when alone. Life will get sweeter when you stand your ground no matter who's around.

Caramel
If you scored 13–16 points, you're made of caramel. You usually stick to your beliefs. But when the heat is on, you go soft. With a little effort, you'll soon discover when to harden up and when to show your soft side.

Jawbreaker
If you scored 17–20 points, you're a jaw-breaker. Jawbreakers are all fun and great— till someone breaks a tooth. It's good to be strong, but if you eat away a little of that hard outer shell, you'll still be plenty tough.

Sixteen Starlets

We're talking fame, fortune, beauty, and boys—aww yeah! Who *wouldn't* want to be a diva—if only for a day? If you could choose to live the life of any ONE of the celebutants listed here, whose would it be? Wait, wait, not so fast! You've gotta do it *right*. Pick a winner from each pair and keep working through the brackets until you have only one name left. That's it! You'll have determined the one starlet *you'd* trade places with (if we twisted your arm, of course).

Britney Spears
vs.
Madonna

Halle Berry
vs.
Mya

Mandy Moore
vs.
Pink

Natalie Portman
vs.
Reese Witherspoon

Gwen Stefani
vs.
Jennifer Lopez

Beyoncé Knowles
vs.
LeAnn Rimes

Sarah Michelle Gellar
vs.
Cameron Diaz

Alicia Keys
vs.
Shakira

Britney Spears
Quarter-finalist

Halle Berry
Quarter-finalist

Halle Berry
Semi-finalist

Pink
Quarter-finalist

Reese Witherspoon
Quarter-finalist

Pink
Semi-finalist

Pink
Finalist

"Just standing around looking beautiful is boring, really boring, so boring."
—Michelle Pfeiffer, actor

Jennifer Lopez
Quarter-finalist

Beyoncé
Quarter-finalist

JLo
Semi-finalist

Sarah Michelle
Quarter-finalist

Shakira
Quarter-finalist

Shakira
Semi-finalist

JLo
Finalist

Pink
The Celeb Life for Me!!!

Girl Stuff Whodunnit

However small or large your girl group is, it's got tons of personality. So, tell us, who's who in your group of girlfriends? (Alternate play: Take a vote among your friends, and supply certificates of recognition for the winners of each category!)

Who always completes her school projects first?_____

Who's always first in line for lunch?_____

Who's had a secret crush?_____

Who takes the cake for having the most embarrassing moment?_____

Who secretly likes something totally "uncool"?_____

Who is the biggest knickknack collector?_____

Who has the most brothers and sisters?_____

Who's always first to know what's fresh and new?_____

Who watches the most TV?_____

Who's the girl with the busiest schedule?_____

Who tells the best jokes?_____

Who wins the most academic awards?_____

Who smiles ALL the time?_____

Who has the cutest giggle?_____

Who is destined to be famous?_____

Who always takes a great school pic?_____

Who has the coolest clothes?_____

Who ALWAYS has something nice to say?_____

Who's the best athlete?_____

Who has the nicest parents?_____

"Be who you are and say what you feel, because those who mind, don't matter and those who matter, don't mind."
—Dr. Seuss, children's book author

Take a Number

All right, so you probably want to be a scientist or a firefighter or something really cool like that when you grow up, right? But let's just say that fate stepped in and decided you would have the ultimate chick career. *The ultimate chick career?!* You betcha! C'mon, just humor us long enough to fill out your numerical 411 on these pages. Then flip the page to discover your true career calling—you won't be disappointed!

What's Your Number?

Average night's sleep (in hours)_____

Your lucky number_____

Your age (in years)_____

Amount of coinage in your piggy bank_____

Total number of times you've (ever) wished you were older_____

Number of pairs of shoes you own_____

Number of pairs of earrings you own_____

Number of crushes you've had in your lifetime_____

Current allowance (in dollars)_____

Hours you've spent daydreaming about becoming famous_____

Number of boys you've really talked with (besides brothers)_____

Hours of TV you watch per week_____

Number of pets that live with you_____

Minutes you spend getting ready for school_____

Number of A's on your last report card_____

Number of brothers and sisters_____

Number of brothers and sisters you actually like to hang with_____

Age you'd like to be_____

Number of posters you have on your wall_____

Number of nail polish colors you own_____

Average time spent studying on the weekend_____

Total_____

Scoring

Add up your total. Then add the digits together until they form a single digit, as shown below.

Example:
Total = 1769
Add digits together: 1+7+6+9 = 23
Add digits together again till you get a single digit: 2+3 = 5
Now flip the page to find out what the digit means!

Career Destiny

Find the job number that matches your final digit from the previous page—then read all about your future fate. (Hey, it could totally happen!)

1. Pediatrician

Oh baby, baby! You'll look super wearing crisp hospital whites and staying calm in a crisis. Plus you'll adore being around all those cute little baby faces!

2. Travel Agent

You have a knack for matching a person with a place. When you're cruisin' together, you'll keep nervous travelers' fears at bay—and helping them fly away pays a nice cash return!

3. Movie Star

You always knew you were meant to be adored. You were destined to handle the attention—and the cash. And then there's the REAL perk: all the super-cute leading men!

4. European Princess

You'll be a well-bred, well-dressed, international beauty. Forget the prince—it's the globe-trotting, feasting, dancing, and dressing up that you love. Oh yeah, and the tiara.

"If I could have any job in the world, I'd be a professional Cinderella."
—Angelina Jolie, actor
(as "Lisa" in the movie *Girl, Interrupted*)

5.
Veterinarian
Sure, you could've been a famous horse trainer, but who wants to spend every day in the tack room? As a vet, you can take care of creatures big and small . . . and still ride the horsies!

6.
Prima Ballerina
You'll be just too-too darling in a fluffy tutu! You'll also get to travel, be the object of every girl's envy, and dance like an angel. It's like a fairy tale!

7.
Preschool Teacher
Tiny tots with their eyes all aglow will be thrilled to see you as their teacher each morning! Plus who else gets paid to sing "The Itsy Bitsy Spider"?!

8.
Interior Designer
Your parent-influenced bedroom digs may not show it, but there's an "ar-teest" inside you. You were meant to remake lives with paint, furniture, and a few expensive trinkets.

9.
Olympic Skater
Even Michelle Kwan won't be able to mimic your triple-axle—that's how good you'll be! Bonus: You can start a whole collection of Wheaties boxes with your pic on them.

Girl Talk

We know you're a natural-born chat-a-holic, but sometimes you just gotta keep your girl talk hush-hush! You can make sure *only* your best buds understand what you're saying by talking in secret code. Try some of the following silly languages to keep your chit-chat super private!

Pig Latin
Pig Latin is pretty common as far as code-speak goes. To speak it, move the first letter of each word to the end of that word and add "ay" (pronounced like the word *hay*).

Example:
"Girls are the best" becomes *Irlsgay are-eay hetay estbay.*

Here are some more variations along the same lines.

Skimono Jive
Add "sk" to the beginning of every word.
Skgirls skare skthe skbest.

Na-Na-Na
Add "na" to the end of every word.
Girlsna arena thena bestna.

Turkey Irish
Add "ab" before every vowel.
Gabirls abarabe thabe babest.

Eggy-Peggy
Add "egg" before each vowel.
Geggirls eggaregge thegge beggest.

The Write Stuff

You also can *write* in secret codes. (That way if somebody else gets hold of your notes, it won't prove so embarrassing!) The easiest way to write in code is to use weird word spacing. First decide on a number of spaces (say, four), and then write your message in code.

For example, instead of
"Meet me by the swings at recess."

You would write:
Meet meby thes wing satr eces s.

Sometimes, like the example above, the letters don't split evenly into groups of four. That's when you add extra letters, called "nulls," to the beginning or end of your message to make it fit the code format.

Wywm eetm ebyt hesw ings atre cess.

The "w" and the "y" at the beginning fill up the extra spaces and make the message harder to decode, so ONLY your girlfriends who know the code will understand the secret message! *Wyws weet!*

It's a Girl Thing

The Friendship Quiz

Are you the girl who gives your friends a shoulder to cry on? Sound advice?
A helping hand? Take this quick quiz to find out all about your friendship style!

1. You and your gal pals go together like

    a. cats and dogs.   b. salt and pepper.   c. PB and J.   d. sugar and spice.

2. You spend as much time IM-ing the girls as you do

    a. working on homework.   c. brushing your hair.
    b. slumbering in dreamland.   d. talking on the phone.

3. After school, you play it cool by

    a. finding some alone time—wherever.   c. spending time at your best chica's house.
    b. chillin' out at home with your fam.   d. joining school-sponsored activities.

4. To you, community service is something

    a. huh?! community *what?*   c. we all should do more.
    b. to do every now and again.   d. that's a big part of day-to-day life.

5. What's in your book bag? (Circle all that apply.)

    a. books (duh!)   e. stationery   i. homework
    b. pencil   f. lip gloss   j. photos of friends
    c. gel pen   g. hairbrush   k. party invitations
    d. stickers   h. notes from friends   l. colored pencils or markers

Scoring

For questions 1–4, award 1 point for each "a," 2 points for each "b," 3 points for each "c," and 4 points for each "d." For question 5, award one point for every answer circled. Now tally up your score!

True Blue

If you scored 4–11, you're true blue to just one buddy. Sure, there are other girls you talk to and hang out with now and again, but it's your BFF who knows you like no one else. You prove your loyalty to her by being available to talk—or listen—24/7, no questions asked. Yeah, you like your alone time, but you're happiest when you're with your best bud. And with a dependable friend like you, why *wouldn't* she stick around forever and ever?

Balanced Groove

If you scored 12–20, you've got your own groove going on, but you love to hang with your crew as well. You're totally flexible—and happy to go from sharing stories with one friend to stealing the spotlight in a large group, all in the blink of an eye. You *do* get bored easily, which causes you to seek out new company and different experiences. But even boredom won't keep you from offering a shoulder to lean on when ANY of your friends need it!

Social Butterfly

If you scored 21–28, *hel-lo* social butterfly! You love to be the center of the social universe. But when a girl's got a jillion-and-one friends to dish the dirt with, it's hard to be there for everyone. You manage to be all ears when a friend has a serious prob, but it's harder to keep up with your pals' day-to-day lives. You might want to slow down just a tad so that you can enjoy some of your closer friendships—even when your friends *don't* have issues.

"Growing up, I was the plain one. I had no style. I was the tough kid with the comb in the back pocket and the feathered hair."
—Cameron Diaz, actor

Sixteen Who Make the Scene

So your girlfriends are your girl-friends because, well, you like hanging out with them and everything. But what if you could add one more girl to your groovy group—one who had all sorts of cool perks and connections and stuff? Choose one celebrity from each pair below and keep playing until there's just one name left. The last celebrity standing is the girl you'd select as your new famous friend!

Kirsten Dunst
vs.
Julia Stiles

Kelly Osbourne
vs.
Christina Aguilera

Ashanti
vs.
Solange Knowles

Michelle Branch
vs.
Vanessa Carlton

Kristin Kreuk
vs.
Ann Hathaway

Beverly Mitchell
vs.
Michelle Trachtenberg

Venus Williams
vs.
Michelle Kwan

Ashley Olsen
vs.
Mary-Kate Olsen

Kirsten Dunst
Quarter-finalist

Christina A.
Quarter-finalist

Christina A.
Semi-finalist

Ashanti'
Quarter-finalist

Vanessa
Quarter-finalist

Vanessa
Semi-finalist

Vanessa
Finalist

Kristen Kreuk
Quarter-finalist

Beverly
Quarter-finalist

Beverly
Semi-finalist

Michelle
Quarter-finalist

Mary-Kate
Quarter-finalist

Mary-Kate
Semi-finalist

Mary-Kate
Finalist

Mary-Kate Olsen
My New Best Friend!

"I always feel like a goofy little kid."
–Julia Stiles, actor

Write On . . .

Did you know that you can interpret your handwriting to discover all sorts of far-out stuff about yourself? If it sounds a little too funky to be true, you'll have to check it out for yourself. Let's see what secrets your scribbles spill!

Copy this sentence in the space below: I couldn't live without ice cream.

Under Pressure!
Study the force of your writing to discover your intensity level.

Light pressure
You're sensitive and forgiving (in fact, you hate fighting!), and you always find the right words to say how you feel.

Heavy pressure
A creative and energetic tornado like you makes a great leader and a loyal friend. Once you decide to get something done, you're halfway there.

Normal, varying pressure
Your energy level rises and falls in a healthy flow. Most of the time, your 'tude is upbeat and you dish solid advice to friends.

Study That Slant

Find out how well you bond with others and how you feel about yourself. (Note: The stronger the slant, the stronger that personality trait will be.)

Left-leaning

At parties, you're: The shy wallflower
Your social circle is: Small and close, with one best friend
Can't go a day without: Daydreaming, being creative, spending time alone

Right-leaning

At parties, you're: At the center of the hubbub
Your social circle is: Huge and spread out, and everyone in it confides in you
Can't go a day without: Thinking about the future, smiling, chit-chatting

Straight up and down

At parties, you're: On the quiet porch, chillin' with a few friends
Your social circle is: Lots o' friendly acquaintances and a few best-best friends
Can't go a day without: Being honest, doing your own thing

More Scribble Secrets

What Nice "I"s You Have

Find the "i" most like yours and decode its meaning.

Round, centered dot ı
You are: Calm, steady
Future calling: Name-on-a-grain-of-rice writer by day, ER surgeon by night

Circle dot i
You are: Artsy, independent
Future calling: A mime who who doubles as an inspirational speaker

Dash dot ī
You are: Curious, spirited
Future calling: Cheerleading captain who also works for the FBI

Round dot to right i
You are: Super aware, always thinking ahead
Future calling: Psychic stockbroker

No dot ı
You are: Waaay relaxed
Future calling: Professional tanner and mattress tester

Decode Your Doodles

Need another reason to shield your notes from prying eyes? Your doodles reveal as much about you as your words do! Here are some of the conclusions others can draw about you based on your ink and pencil scribbles.

Squares or patterns
Efficient and organized

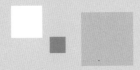

Circles
Honest and a people person

Stars, arrows, ladders
Optimistic and ambitious

House
Desire for a peaceful home life

Flowers
Tender and protective

Hearts
Sweet and thoughtful

"The real secret to gorgeousness is to believe in yourself, have self-confidence, and try to be secure in your decisions and thoughts."
—Kirsten Dunst, actor

Who Knows You Best?

Secretly you're just dying to know how well your friends and family *really* know you, right? Here's an easy way to find out! Fill out the info in the first column yourself. Then interview people you're tight with to see who knows your likes and dislikes. (Fill out the form yourself so they can't cheat by peeking at your answers!)

	Me	My BFF	My mom
My favorite TV show			
The brand name I love			
My shoe size			
The CD I play most			
My fave saying			
The best gift I ever got			
My all-time favorite subject			
The career I want to have			
I can't wait to travel to			
The food I'm addicted to			

Total number correct guesses _____ _____

My sister/cousin	My pet	My classmate	My neighbor

Lunchroom BINGO

Want a cool way to get stoked about mystery meat? Need a way to spice up those unexciting PB-and-J days? We have the solution: LUNCH! No, no, not the meal, silly. We mean the game. Follow the rules below to get a head start on recess.

Here's how you play:

1. Make a copy of the game board for every player, including yourself.
2. Each player creates her own game board from the items list (below) by writing or drawing one choice in each square (except the center square—it's FREE!). Players are not allowed to choose items from the list that they KNOW they have in their lunchbox!!! (Anyone caught cheating has to bring cookies for the whole group the next day.)
3. When any player spots an item from the game board in the lunchroom, she notifies the group. If the group agrees that the item is a match, anyone who has that item on her board gets to mark it off.
4. As in BINGO, the first player to "Connect 5" wins. You determine the prize (but we're thinking a special lunch prepared by the group would be awfully nice—one day free from caf food for your friend!).

Lunchroom BINGO board items:

mystery meat	PB and J	juice box	fruit snacks	boxed raisins
white bread	pizza	pretzels	apple	note from Mom
burrito	carrot sticks	pink napkin	cheeseburger	chocolate milk
applesauce	ketchup	lunch tray	boiled egg	sugar cookie
potato chips	peas	string cheese	brown napkin	note from Dad
pudding pack	crackers	soda	green gelatin	fruit cocktail
deli sandwich	soup	tuna	rice	chocolate snack

"Green Eggs and Ham was the story of my life. I wouldn't eat a thing when I was a kid, but Dr. Suess inspired me to try cauliflower." –Jim Carrey, actor

L	U	N	C	H
		FREE		

Fortune Finders

Bake, Hunt, and Win

OK, you've been going on treasure hunts since you were, what, 3? But that doesn't mean they're not a blast. And you never need an excuse for hide-n-seek fun!

Here's what you do:

1. Determine a prize for the winners, such as a cool new journal, a chart-topping CD, or a "gift certificate" for an afternoon of study help.

2. Figure out the best hiding places in your house and some clues that will lead you to them. Then use a nontoxic pen to write the clues on small strips of paper—about 2-1/2" x 1/2" (6.5 x 1.5 cm). On each back, write the number of the clue. Fold the papers lengthwise (number side out).

3. Invite your girl group over to bake (see recipe at right). But be sure nobody peeks at the clues!

4. Hide the cookies. Happy hunting!

Finders' Cookies

These finders' cookies taste just like their cousins—fortune cookies—but what's inside makes ALL the difference. (Tip: Ask Grandma, Mom, or an older sis for help baking.)

Finders' Cookies Recipe

- 1 large egg white
- 1/4 cup (60 ml) sugar
- 1/4 cup (60 ml) all-purpose flour
- 1/8 teaspoon (0.5 ml) vanilla extract

1. Preheat the oven to 400°F (200°C) and grease two cookie sheets.
2. Whisk together the egg white and vanilla until foam forms. Blend in the flour and sugar until smooth.
3. Spoon batter onto the baking sheets—about 2 teaspoons (10 ml) for each cookie, spaced well apart. Bake until the edges are golden (about 5 minutes).
4. Remove the cookies and flop them upside down on wax paper.
5. IMPORTANT: Before you place a clue inside a cookie, note its number!
6. Place each clue in the center of a warm cookie, and fold each cookie in half. Bend the pointed edges toward each other, and place the cookie in a cup or round cookie cutter to hold the shape.
7. When the cookies cool, wrap each one in foil. Mark the clue number on the outside.

Where've YOU Been?

True Identity Quiz

Not that we believe in this stuff, but we heard from a reliable source that you were *something else* in a previous life. Want to find out more? You'll have to take this quiz to discover your history (or is it *her*-story?)!

1. You'd describe your best physical feature as

   a. your bright, pretty eyes.
   b. your perfectly polished nails.
   c. your big, flashy smile.
   d. your ultra-glamorous hair.

2. Your worst nightmare is to be stranded

   a. on a deserted island.
   b. at school.
   c. in a jungle.
   d. at home alone.

3. You wish every movie included this "type" of character:

   a. the jock.   b. the rebel.   c. the artist.   d. the brainiac.

4. Of the following colors, you prefer

   a. yellow.   b. green.   c. orange.   d. blue.

5. Which scenario would make you happiest?

   a. winning the lottery
   b. winning a popularity contest
   c. winning a Nobel Prize
   d. winning an Oscar or Grammy

Scoring

1. a = 1, b = 2, c = 3, d = 4   2. a = 1, b = 2, c = 4, d = 3   3. a = 4, b = 3, c = 2, d = 1
4. a = 3, b = 4, c = 1, d = 2   5. a = 2, b = 4, c = 1, d = 3

Purr-fectly Fur-ocious Personality

If you scored 5–8, in your past life, you were Princess the Tiger. Don't let the frou-frou name fool you; you were one tough tigress. Now, Princess, you didn't spend days hanging out with the "in" kitty crowd, soaking up gossip and sunshine. Oh, no! You were super busy even as a young cub, when you started pulling your weight in the animal kingdom by saving up allowances for Save the Animals funds. Heck, your tiger eyes were always focused on the future, which is where the phrase "Go get 'em, Tiger!" comes from!

Tough Shell, Soft Inside

If you scored 9–12, in your past life, you were Pinky the Turtle. You had stars in her eyes and nail polish on your shell. Let's just say you'd stand out in any crowd, even without the cotton-candy colored outside. As Pinky, you were a legend among turtles because you never forgot one super-important lesson: Others come first. You were always there with a tissue or an LOL joke—ready for an absolute sobfest or a super-hard laugh at a moment's notice. When you were Pinky, you were much more than just a pretty face: You were a model friend.

Serious about Monkey Business

If you scored 13–17, in your past life, you were Sassy the Monkey. You thought your life was a circus—and you were right! As Sassy, you were a primate with sparkle and pizzazz—and what better place for you to shine than under the Big Top? You traveled around the world performing amazing acrobatics for awestruck audiences. But unlike lots of big stars, you totally had the whole fame thing under control. You were all about giving back in any way that you could. Thank you, thank you, and a million more thanks—from your fans!

Logging a Lot of Laughs

If you scored 18–20, in your past life, you were Giggles the Woodchuck. When you were Giggles, you were into being popular, but not in a bad way or anything. You just really loved making friends with the new kid, keeping up on all the latest and greatest news and happenings, and telling positively *everyone* you knew about *what* you knew. As Giggle, you were really happiest when you were playing hostess to a dam-full of family and friends—who were always coming to visit your ultra-hip neck of the woods. Giggles, you were glam *and* great!

Sixteen Crush Candidates

Whether you scream "AAAAHHHHH!!!! JOSH HARTNETT! JOSH HARTNETT!" or dream about becoming a princess, this game is for you. Select only one name from each set of celebrity cuties, and keep playing through the brackets till you have just one name left. You may be surprised by the "crush of your life" you choose in the end!

> "Marry Prince William?
> I would love that. After all,
> who wouldn't want to be a princess?"
> —Britney Spears, pop star

Josh Hartnett
vs.
Casey Affleck

Hayden Christiansen
vs.
Justin Timberlake

Freddie Prinze, Jr.
vs.
Joshua Jackson

Tobey Maguire
vs.
Kobe Bryant

Shane West
vs.
Aaron Carter

Prince William
vs.
Prince Harry

Ashton Kutcher
vs.
Ashley Angel

Frankie Muniz
vs.
Seth Green

Josh Hartnett
Quarter-finalist

Hayden Christiansen
Semi-finalist

Hayden Christiansen
Quarter-finalist

Hayden Christiansen
Finalist

Freddie Prinze Jr.
Quarter-finalist

Tobey Maguire
Semi-finalist

Tobey Maguire
Quarter-finalist

Ashton Kutcher
My Ultimate
Crush-ola!

Aaron Carter
Quarter-finalist

Prince William
Semi-finalist

Prince William
Quarter-finalist

Ashton Kutcher
Finalist

Ashton Kutcher
Quarter-finalist

Ashton Kutcher
Semi-finalist

Frankie Muniz
Quarter-finalist

Nail-Biters

Sometimes the choices we're given are between something "bad" and something "even worse." If you had to choose the worst option from each pair, which would it be? (Mark the answers you choose to avoid!)

Which is worse . . .

- ☐ eating cafeteria lunches or ☐ having to prepare your own lunches?
- ☐ being sick on the weekend or ☐ being well on a test day?
- ☐ snoring at a sleepover or ☐ talking in your sleep?
- ☐ finding a spider in your salad or ☐ finding a centipede in your shower?
- ☐ falling asleep at school or ☐ having a dream about school?
- ☐ staying late after school or ☐ arriving late to school?
- ☐ taking the bus or ☐ missing the bus?
- ☐ wearing mismatching shoes or ☐ wearing PJs to school?
- ☐ having your mom read your diary or ☐ having your teacher read your notes?
- ☐ forgetting your schoolwork at home or ☐ forgetting your homework at school?
- ☐ being at home ill on the day of a field trip or ☐ getting sick while on a field trip?

"Everybody wants to go to a club or watch a movie,
and I have to stay home and do homework. How is that fair?"
—Mandy Moore, singer and actor
(on her concert tour experiences)

Girl with the Most Cake

Sometimes you want to have your cake and eat it too. If you had to choose between these AWESOME circumstances, which would you take? (Mark the answers you want the most!)

Which is better . . .

☐ having X-ray vision or ☐ being able to fly?

☐ sleeping all day or ☐ staying up all night?

☐ having no school due to snow or ☐ getting out of school for a holiday?

☐ vacationing at the beach or ☐ spending your holiday at a winter retreat?

☐ being on summer vacation or ☐ getting out for spring break?

☐ earning straight A's or ☐ never receiving a report card?

☐ discovering a "just because" gift in the mail or ☐ finding money on the sidewalk?

☐ being given a brand new bicycle NOW or ☐ being guaranteed a new car when you turn 16?

☐ being able to read minds or ☐ being able to predict the future?

☐ never having to do homework again or ☐ never having to do chores again?

☐ being offered a contract to write a book or ☐ being offered a chance to record an album?

☐ snacking on raw cookie dough or ☐ devouring still-warm, freshly baked cookies?

It's a Charmed Life

Good luck can follow you everywhere, especially if you attach it! Mold your own lucky charm out of clay, using the recipe at right, and then wear it for good luck. You can lace it through your shoelaces, carry it in your pocket, fashion it into a charm bracelet or necklace, or even make it into a key ring! Choose charms for your girlfriends too—give them as gifts, or glue them to framed pictures of your buddies to bring your friends good fortune!

Lucky Charms

Symbol	Meaning
arrow	health
bear	strength
cat	vision
dolphin	safe travel
dove	peace
dragon	happiness
fish	wealth
frog	friendship
lion	courage
owl	knowledge
pyramid	energy
key	opportunity
snake	love
sun	fame
turtle	creativity
unicorn	safety
wishbone	dreams come true

arrow

bear

dove

dragon

cat

key

lion

fish

unicorn

wishbone

sun

turtle

owl

snake

pyramid

dolphin

frog

No-Bake Clay Recipe

- 2 cups (500 ml) baking soda
- 1-1/4 cups (310 ml) cold water
- 1 cup (250 ml) cornstarch

1. Mix the clay ingredients in a 2-quart (2 L) saucepan. Ask an adult to help you cook it over medium heat, stirring constantly until the mixture has a pastelike texture.

2. Pour the moist dough onto a piece of aluminum foil, and cover it with a damp dishtowel until cool. But don't let it harden yet!

3. To add color, take a small amount of clay and add drops of food coloring (any color you like). Wearing rubber gloves, knead the clay until the color is evenly spread out. Roll the clay into 1/2" (1.5 cm) balls, and shape them to match the charm of your choice. Then let the clay air dry for 2–3 days.

What It Feels Like . . . for a Girl

It can be tough to be a girl in today's world—just ask mega-girl stars like Madonna or Gwen Stefani, who even wrote songs about what it's like! What are they talking about? Find out when you play this board game.

The Rules

1. Use coins to mark your progress on the game board.
2. Roll a die to determine who goes first. The lowest roller begins.
3. Player 1 rolls the die and advances that number of spaces. She follows the directions on her square and then passes on play to the next player.
4. Each time a player lands on a new square on her journey to day's end, she earns a point.
5. If a player lands on a square with a terrible, awful, no good, unlucky scenario that she's actually experienced in real life, she earns two additional points.
6. The player with the most points at game's end is in need of Lady Luck's company the most, so she's the winner. Pamper her with some friendly hugs and words of encouragement!

Start

Bad Hair Day
Your curls came out looking more Shirley Temple than Keri Russell. Go back to Start.

Bus Stop Blues
Choosing the perfect pair of shoes is hard when you're rushed! Miss the bus, skip a turn.

What Homework?!
You were so stoked about a TV special that you forgot about social studies.
Go forward 2.

Pigtail Pull
The boy behind you in science class won't stop tugging at your too-cute 'tails.

Pink Cheeked
Leave it to Grandma—she sends you a training bra via mail. And you open it in front of your dad!

Blindfold, Please?
You hit the kitchen for a snack but find Mom and Dad kissing! Um, gross?! Go forward 1.

Mom-to-Dot
Mom wants to have a little talk with you about . . . well, you know. Go back 1.

Tie-Breaker
You bend down to tie your shoelace in the middle of a big game, and find it snapped in two!

Roller Tears
You hit a slippery spot on the crowded skating rink. As you do the splits, so do your pants!

Math Problem
Math class was fine till you got sick—and only made it as far as the trash can. Skip a turn.

The End
Even with all the yucky stuff, you made it to day's end. Tomorrow will be better—promise!

Doodle Reader
Your daydream becomes a nightmare when your crush spies his name in your heart scribbles.

"Do you know what it feels like for a girl? Do you know what it feels like in this world, for a girl?"
–Madonna, singer
("What It Feels Like for a Girl")

Soppy Situation
Your lunch drink spills and leaves an embarrassing stain on your shirt. Go forward 1.

Where's the Sock?
One sock too few in PE class is like, well, going barefoot in the locker room. Eww!

Hall Pass
You get caught passing notes—and get sent to the principal as "an example." Go back 2.

Little Sneak
Your little bro reads your diary from cover to cover while you're at school.

Truly Crushed
You discover that your secret crush is secretly crushing on someone else!

Minus One

Ever dream about what it would be like if you ruled the world of entertainment? If you HAD to remove one person or character from each category—even though you like EVERYBODY—who would it be? (Alternate: Play with your friends. The characters with the most votes get ousted—unless you can provide reasons to make them stay!)

7th Heaven _____

Dawson's Creek _____

Friends _____

'N Sync _____

Backstreet Boys _____

Lizzie McGuire _____

State of Grace _____

Malcolm in the Middle _____

Gilmore Girls _____

Smallville _____

Sabrina, the Teenage Witch _____

The Princess Diaries _____

Harry Potter series_____

SpongeBob SquarePants_____

Sagwa, the Chinese Siamese Cat _____

Destiny's Child _____

Scooby-Doo!_____

"Here's to the future! The only limits are the limits of our imagination. Dream up the kind of world you want to live in, dream out loud, at high volume."
—Bono, singer and member of rock band U2

What's Your Flavor?

Popsicle Personality Quiz

What's more chill than a celebrity party? Brighter than a team of quiz contestants? More popular than ice cream in summer? Popsicles! And since everybody knows you're so sweet you could put sugar out of business, we think this quiz is a perfect fit. Find out your personal flavor by answering a few simple questions.

1. When alone at home, you're most likely to

    a. boogie around the house to some favorite jams.
    b. get your homework done without distractions.
    c. practice your oh-so-sweet singing voice.
    d. channel-surf the tube while the remote is yours, *all* yours.

2. If you could choose to study only one subject this year, it would be

    a. social studies. b. math. c. science. d. reading.

3. You tend to daydream about your summer vacations plans

    a. at least a year ahead. c. whenever the subject comes up.
    b. a few months in advance. d. on the last day of school, at the earliest.

4. If you had to pick one food to eat for a week straight, it'd be

    a. burgers. b. chips 'n' dip. c. pizza. d. salad.

5. The one modern convenience you simply couldn't live without is

    a. the telephone. b. electricity. c. the microwave. d. running water.

Scoring

If you answered mostly a's, your personality is **Cherry** flavored. Yeah, yeah, Cherry may seem like a pretty standard flavor and all, but a Cherry personality is anything but typical. Your lovable laughter and your strong sense of style make you a standout even in a super-crowded pack. You were born to add color and excitement to an otherwise dull and flavor-challenged world!

If you answered mostly b's, your personality is **Grape** flavored. Grape is the classic flavor we all love. Why, you ask? Because Grapes are smart and dependable. You may not be lovin' your super-nice girl status, but others are tickled purple that you're not full of surprises. Friends choose you because you never spill their secrets and you know how to deal with, well, whatever!

If you answered mostly c's, your personality is **Lime** flavored. Lime, we're green with envy over your oh-so-amazing personality. You're the only person we know who *always* plays by her own rules, does what feels right *when* it feels right, and *doesn't* worry about being everyone else's favorite. Others are drawn to the lime-light glow of your unique character—naturally!

If you answered mostly d's, your personality is **Orange** flavored. Orange, we don't want to say that you're the *player* of the group, but you're definitely the playful spirit! With your can-do attitude and always-sweet, never-sour personality, no one will ever accuse you of being the stick in the Popsicle. Instead your outgoing character means you're never one friend shy of a twin-pack.

CELEB

Can't get enough of celebrities? Got a stack of cool mags in a corner collecting dust? Like to be entertained AND in-the-know? Then you're ready for CELEB!

Here's how you play:

1. Make a copy of the game board for every player, including yourself.
2. Grab scissors and some magazines and start cutting out pics of fave celebrities. (Tip: Clip pics small enough to fit in the squares.)
3. Each player creates a game board, pasting a celeb pic in every square. (Each celeb can appear only once per board—so forget about dedicating the entire board to Justin.)
4. On small strips of paper, write the names of all the celebrities whose pics have been used. Place the names in a hat or bowl for drawing.
5. One by one, pull names and read them aloud. Just as in BINGO, mark off the celebs on your board as they're called. The first player to "Connect 5" wins (drum roll, please) . . . a date with her celebrity crush!!! (Um, or not. How 'bout she wins a poster of him you've all pitched in to buy?)

C	E	L	E	B
		FREE		

Crazy Eights and Double Trouble

We've all daydreamed about who we'd like to hook up (and who we'd like to break up), so here's your chance to pick out a super-couple. Nominate 8 females and 8 males (from Hollywood, books, the news, sports, *wherever*), and write their names down in alphabetical order on the lines provided. Then choose one name from each pair of names until you're left with only one guy and one girl—the ultimate power pair!

"I always admired Wonder Woman and the Incredible Hulk . . ."
—Lucy Liu, actor

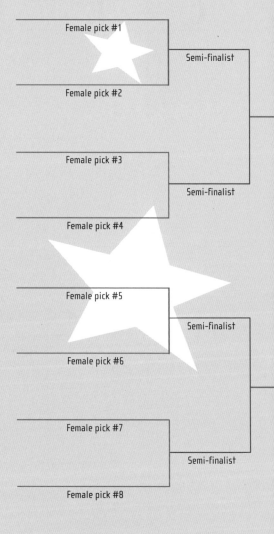

Female pick #1

Semi-finalist

Female pick #2

Female pick #3

Semi-finalist

Female pick #4

Female pick #5

Semi-finalist

Female pick #6

Female pick #7

Semi-finalist

Female pick #8

Fill in your 8 female picks above (in alpha order)

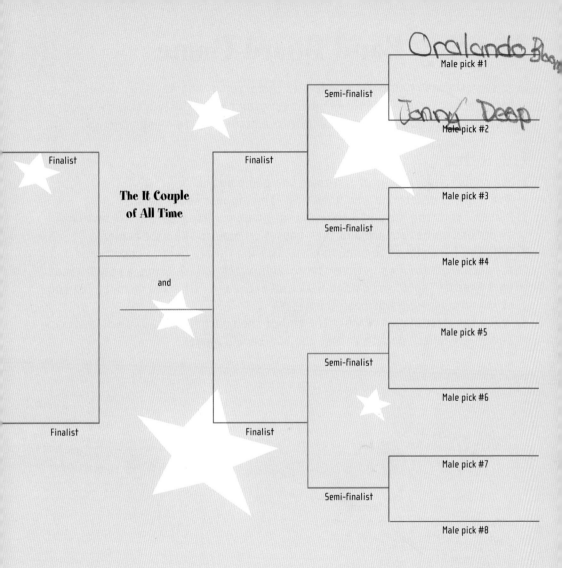

Finalist

**The It Couple
of All Time**

and

Finalist

Finalist

Semi-finalist

Finalist

Semi-finalist

Semi-finalist

Finalist

Semi-finalist

Oralando Bloom
Male pick #1

Janny Deep
Male pick #2

Male pick #3

Male pick #4

Male pick #5

Male pick #6

Male pick #7

Male pick #8

Fill in your 8 male picks above
(in alpha order)

The Boy Band Board Game

Ever secretly wish you could preview all those super-talented (and cute!) guys before the boy bands are chosen? Well now *you* can be the judge! Here's your chance to create your own boy band, with a little help from your friends.

The Rules

1. Use coins to mark your progress on the game board.
2. Roll a die to determine who goes first. The highest roller begins.
3. Player 1 rolls the die and advances that number of spaces. She follows the directions on her square and then passes on play to the next player.
4. Only the first player to land on each "Casting" space gets to choose one band member from the two options shown. *But watch out!* Anytime a player lands on a "Recast" spot, she can go back and exchange ONE band member for any other member who was passed up!
5. When the first player reaches the end of the board, the band is set in stone—and the "winner" gets to choose the boy band's name!

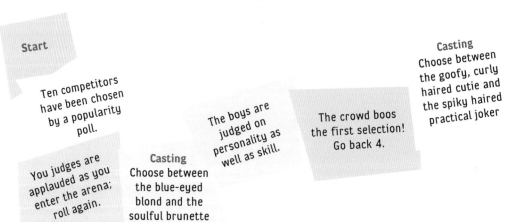

Start

Ten competitors have been chosen by a popularity poll.

You judges are applauded as you enter the arena; roll again.

Casting
Choose between the blue-eyed blond and the soulful brunette

The boys are judged on personality as well as skill.

The crowd boos the first selection! Go back 4.

Casting
Choose between the goofy, curly haired cutie and the spiky haired practical joker

One of the boys on stage winks in your direction! Roll again.

Casting
Choose between the doll-faced baby of the group and the rocker with a rebel attitude

The judges confer over the last casting decision. Skip a turn.

Recast

Casting
Choose between the rockin' guitarist and the "boy next door" drummer

You call your BFF on your cell phone to give her a casting update.

You get caught daydreaming about dating the contestants. Go back 6!

Recast

The crowd goes wild for the judges' last choice. Go forward 2.

Casting
Choose between the hip and rhythmic dancer and the goofy guy with the voice of an angel

One of the newly cast bandmates asks for your name and number. Go forward 2.

The Final Bandmates

_____
_____
_____
_____
_____

Recast

Name the Band

_____

The judges consider the final band arrangement.

Winner!
The casting is complete—now name the newly formed band!!!

A recount of votes is called. Skip a turn.

What Ifs

Sometimes it's worth thinking about things—even if they may never happen. Consider the following "what if" options with your girlfriends and decide which you'd rather do or be. (Mark your preferences.)

Would you rather . . .

- ☐ be a brunette or ☐ be a blond?
- ☐ become a movie star or ☐ become a movie star's girlfriend?
- ☐ excel at sports or ☐ excel at school?
- ☐ be paid the lottery in one lump sum or ☐ be paid over time?
- ☐ own a cat or ☐ own a dog?
- ☐ have one really, really good friend or ☐ have lots of girlfriends?
- ☐ travel to far-away places or ☐ relax at home?
- ☐ hang out with girlfriends or ☐ hang out with your family?
- ☐ eat dinner at a restaurant or ☐ chow down at home?
- ☐ be a kid or ☐ become an adult?
- ☐ become rich (but remain unknown) or ☐ become famous (but not rich)?
- ☐ go skydiving or ☐ go bungee-jumping?
- ☐ live the life of a fairy-tale princess or ☐ live the life of a super model?
- ☐ have a free pass to get out of school or ☐ have a free pass to get out of being sick?

"Sometimes it's the smallest decisions that can change your life forever."
–Keri Russell, actor
(as Felicity, on TV show *Felicity*)

For a Cool Mill

We all know that money isn't everything, but you gotta admit that it sure can provide motivation! How far would you go for a million bucks of cold cash?

	Sure!	No way!	Um, maybe

Would you . . .

- pretend you were an alien for the rest of the school year? ☐ ☐ ☐
- dance by yourself at the next all-school assembly? ☐ ☐ ☐
- read aloud a whole book over the loudspeaker? ☐ ☐ ☐
- eat a bowl full of still wriggling worms? ☐ ☐ ☐
- wink at your crush next time he looks at you? ☐ ☐ ☐
- go without dessert for the rest of your life? ☐ ☐ ☐
- listen only to CDs that your parents pick out? ☐ ☐ ☐
- appear on a reality TV show? ☐ ☐ ☐
- go back in time and live in the 1800s for a year? ☐ ☐ ☐
- trade in your teenage years and go straight from kid to adult? ☐ ☐ ☐
- give up all television watching forever? ☐ ☐ ☐
- kiss a real, live frog? ☐ ☐ ☐
- memorize a new word from the dictionary every day? ☐ ☐ ☐

"Everyone wants to ride with you in the limo, but what you need is someone who will take the bus with you when the limo breaks down."
—Oprah Winfrey, TV talk-show host

Truth or Dare

Here's the truth: There's no fun like basic silliness with your girlfriends. So we dare you to gather your crew and challenge them to an old-fashioned game of courage.

How to Play

1. Determine a prize for the boldest girl in your crew. Make it something really good—like a new CD or movie tickets—because whoever wins is going to have to get pretty gutsy to earn her reward. (Everybody can pitch in the moola when it comes time to buy the prize.)
2. Decide the length of your game time. It can be one hour, one evening, one week, or even one month if you want.
3. Make copies of the dares for whoever wants to play. As soon as everybody's ready, start racking up the points.
4. You earn points for each act of bravery that you accomplish but only if someone witnesses it. Truths are worth 1 point, Dares are worth 3 points, Double Dares are worth 5 points.
5. At the end of the game time, she with the most points wins. Congratulate her on her boldness and present her with her super-cool prize!

Truth

Pay your teacher a compliment—one that you really mean.
Tell your parents five reasons why you appreciate them—in front of witnesses.
Ask your best friend's crush if he likes her back!
Tell at least three people your most embarrassing moment ever.

Dare

Wear mismatching shoes for an entire school day.
On movie night, dress up like a character in the film that you're going to see.
Enter an art or writing competition with one of your original creations.
Try out for a sport you've never played.

Double Dare

Challenge the neighborhood boys to a basketball game against your girl crew.
Loudly belt out a song at recess—the whole song, not just the chorus.
Sit next to a boy on the bus ride to school—or at an all-school assembly.
Eat lunch with a group of classmates you don't know well.

"One of the things that [my mother] loves to reiterate is that the Chinese symbol for 'crisis' means both danger and opportunity." –Ashley Judd, actor

Keeping Score

She did what?!? Tally points for courageous acts here. Don't leave out any details!

Player's name	Date	What she did	Points earned

Winner _____

Star Light, Star Bright

Would You Like to Wish on a Star?

Why wait for a shooting star to make your dreams come true? Check out these funky, poetic ways to wish out loud any ol' day! (But remember: Be careful what you wish for—it just might come true!)

For Good Grades

This one may take a little practice. Standing outside on a starry night (preferably before a big test), balance three textbooks on your head and walk around in a circle. Repeat the rhyme below three times, and then return inside and sleep with the books under your pillow.

> Send the C's and D's away.
> Keep those gnarly F's at bay.
> Oh my lucky stars above,
> It's those A's and B's I love!

For Staying Awake in Class

Here's wishful thinking for those mornings when the school day started too soon (which is, what, like every morning?). When all you want is another hour in your warm, cozy bed and your eyes are starting to shut, repeat this rhyme twice under your breath without blinking.

> Please help me stay awake at school;
> Oversleeping isn't cool.
> Tired, tired, tired is me—
> Open my eyes wide as can be.

For Remembering Things

This is a simple idea for all you girls who make a list of things you need to remember but then lose the list. (You'll like this one. Promise.) First thing in the morning, gather some hard candies, a pencil, and a piece of paper in front of you. With the paper and pencil, make a list of the things you need to remember that day; then place a candy in your pocket for each item you need to remember. Read the rhyme below only once. Then read over your list three times. Keep the candies in your pocket, because every time you remember one of the items on your list, you get to eat a candy. By the end of the day, you should have remembered everything you needed to do, and the candy should be all gone. Your wish will have come true—sweet!

> I've forgotten my homework, my pen, and my book.
> I've forgotten so much that I have a lost look.
> But there is no need to get all in a huff;
> I've got a sweet tooth for remembering stuff!

To Get (or Stay) out of Trouble

Okay, we all know you'd never, ever do something that'd get you grounded. But let's just say that you DID do something and that you need a quick fix to get outta trouble. Try opening and shutting a door as softly as possible as you repeat this rhyme seven times in a whisper.

> Whoops. I admit, I made a mistake;
> Now all my privileges my folks will take.
> Don't want my parents to throw a huge fit:
> Clear me of trouble, and lickety split!

After Hours Are Ours . . .

Who says after school hours have to be *bor*-ing? Here's a whole month of special activities to brighten up your ho-hum afternoons and evenings—um, but only after you finish your homework!!!

Playful "Paws"
Spend some quality time with your favorite furry friends—at home or at a shelter.

Girl Next Door
Bake super-yummy treats for your nicest neighbors.

Step to It
Get the girls together to choreograph a hip dance to your all-time fave jam!

Outta Sight
Girlify your bikes with pretty stuff to parade them around your 'hood!

Music Mania
Flip through your CDs for so-very-you songs for a personalized tape or CD.

Fancy Face
Exchange makeovers with your sister, mom, or very best friend!!!

Time Flies
Bury your girl group's "so last year" stuff in a closet time-capsule.

Olly Olly Oxen Free!
You're never too old to join in a game of tag with the local kidlets.

"My favorite school memory is getting together with all my friends
and going back-to-school shopping for clothes. It's all about the clothes."
—Beverley Mitchell, actor

Chick Fest
Stock up on munchies and invite your crew to a Girls Movie Night.

Easy Reader
Pick a book—any book—and escape with a good read.

Squeaky Clean
Donate the fashionable leftovers from your over-stuffed closet to charity.

Tall Tales
Create a memory book with all your scraps from never-to-forget moments!

Grow Happy
Plant a garden—inside or out—and fill it with sweet-smelling plants.

Dream-a-Design
Redecorate your room in a new color or theme—or just daydream about it.

Surfer Girl
Hop on the web to find the 411 about the places you'd LOVE to visit!

Young at Heart
Gather (a) friends and (b) beauty supplies and offer retirement-home
residents free makeovers!

. . . ALL Ours!!!

Clean Sweep
Sell your junk at a yard sale to make $$$ for Girls-Only activities!

For the Birds
Borrow binoculars and bird-watch. Extra credit: Imitate the calls!

Pick-Me-Up
Host an indoor picnic! Cover the floor with a tablecloth and serve fave warm-weather treats.

X Marks the Spot
Make a map of your 'hood and all it's secret paths and hideaways.
Bonus: Bury a treasure!

Tour Guide
Record a video tour of your home (tell fun stories in each room!)

Holidaze
Create a Girls' holiday. Choose a mascot, decorate with pink and purple, and serve lots of sweets!

Pampered Princess
Take time out with a bubble bath. Think scented oils, sweet-smelling candles, and relaxing tunes.

Girlhood Giggles
Invite an older girl (like your mom) to have a pillow fight, paint toenails, and tell silly stories!

Singin' in the Rain
Don't let a rainy day get you down, or keep you in! Get out and splash in some super mud puddles.

Just Dreamin'
Ask your mom or a neighbor to go through her wedding pictures with you—ask tons of Q's!

Chef in da' House
Cook up a "restaurant-style" meal for your fam, with menus and décor.

Sing It, Baby!
Rewrite the words to your favorite song to describe life with your girl group. Voilà! Instant theme song!

Puzzling Fun
Gather friends to put together a puzzle—but hide the box till it's done!

Stargazers
Get info about constellations and try to find them in the sky.

Role Reversal
Ask a female teacher what it was like to be a girl when she was a kid.

Say Cheese
Pretend you're modeling for a photo shoot and take tons of goofy pics!

"My theory is that if you look confident you can pull off anything—even if you have no clue what you're doing."
—Jessica Alba, actor

You Rock!

Wanna be a rock star? A rap sensation? A divine diva? OK. "Borrow" the talent. Say *what?!* Just write your fave lyrics on some colorful paper or stationery, one word at a time. Use different colors of gel pens or markers, and make the words all different sizes. Then cut the words out in little boxes and rearrange them to create your own slammin' song, rippin' rap, or rhymin' verse. When it's complete, paste down your master-mix all over these two pages, word by word.

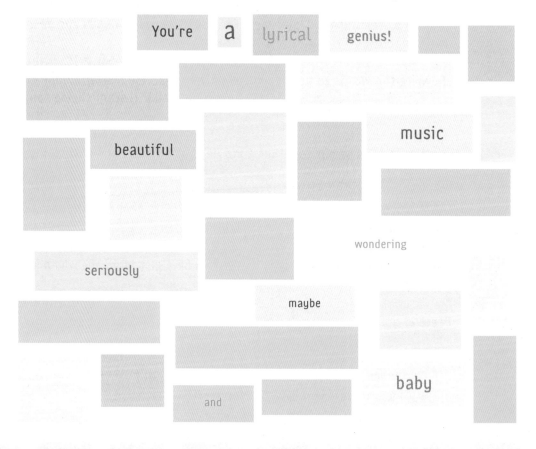

You're a lyrical genius!

beautiful

music

seriously

wondering

maybe

and

baby

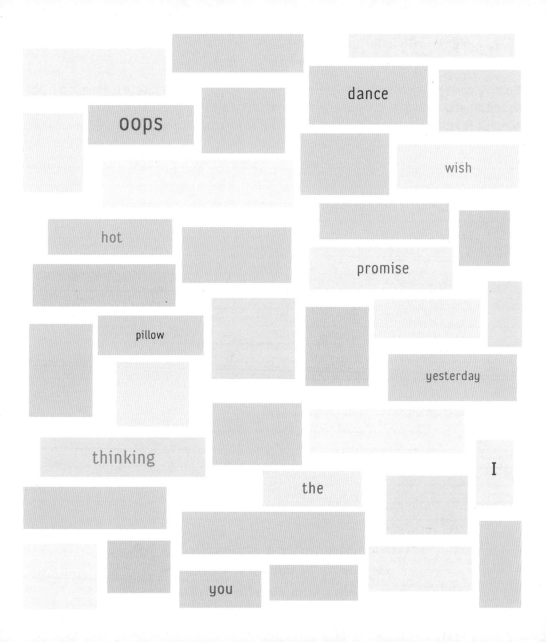

dance

oops

wish

hot

promise

pillow

yesterday

thinking

I

the

you

The Last Word

Nobody can tell you how to be a girl—it's something that you just are. Here's a place to tell all about how girls will be girls—in other people's words! Write and remember all your fave quotes here, whether they're from friends, celebs, books, or teachers.

_____
_____
_____
_____
_____
_____
_____
_____
_____
_____
_____
_____
_____
_____
_____
_____
_____
_____

"I think women are the most courageous people;
they always get through any situation."
–Alicia Keys, singer/songwriter